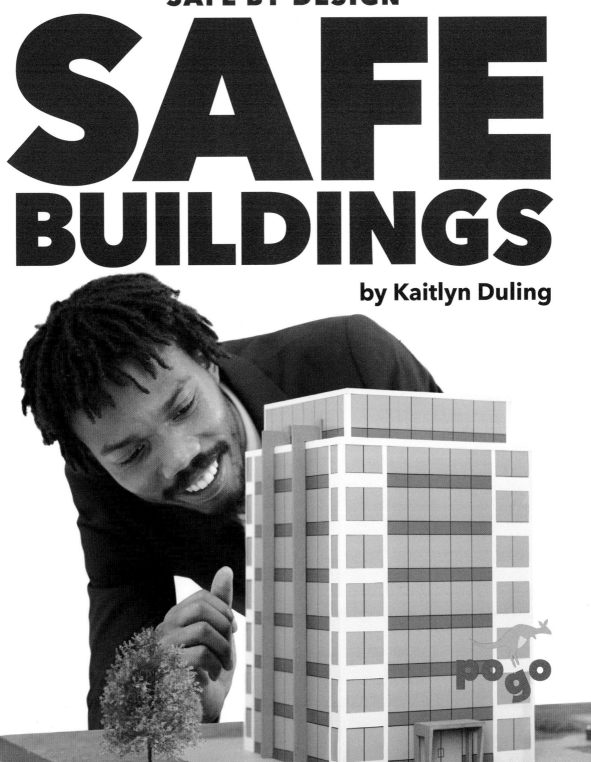

SAFE BY DESIGN

SAFE BUILDINGS

by Kaitlyn Duling

pogo

Ideas for Parents and Teachers

Pogo Books let children practice reading informational text while introducing them to nonfiction features such as headings, labels, sidebars, maps, and diagrams, as well as a table of contents, glossary, and index.

Carefully leveled text with a strong photo match offers early fluent readers the support they need to succeed.

Before Reading

- "Walk" through the book and point out the various nonfiction features. Ask the student what purpose each feature serves.

- Look at the glossary together. Read and discuss the words.

Read the Book

- Have the child read the book independently.

- Invite him or her to list questions that arise from reading.

After Reading

- Discuss the child's questions. Talk about how he or she might find answers to those questions.

- Prompt the child to think more. Ask: Buildings need to be safe from many kinds of natural disasters. What kind of natural disasters happen in your area? How is your home built to withstand them?

Pogo Books are published by Jump!
5357 Penn Avenue South
Minneapolis, MN 55419
www.jumplibrary.com

Library of Congress Cataloging-in-Publication Data

Names: Duling, Kaitlyn, author.
Title: Safe buildings / by Kaitlyn Duling.
Description: Minneapolis, MN: Jump!, Inc., 2020.
Series: Safe by design | Audience: Age 7-10.
Includes bibliographical references and index.
Identifiers: LCCN 2018055806 (print)
LCCN 2018057286 (ebook)
ISBN 9781641288774 (ebook)
ISBN 9781641288750 (hardcover : alk. paper)
ISBN 9781641288767 (pbk. : alk. paper)
Subjects: LCSH: Buildings—Protection—Juvenile literature. | Buildings—Safety measures—Juvenile literature. | Buildings—Safety appliances—Juvenile literature.
Classification: LCC TH9025 (ebook)
LCC TH9025 .D85 2019 (print) | DDC 690/.22—dc23
LC record available at https://lccn.loc.gov/2018055806

Editor: Susanne Bushman
Designer: Anna Peterson

Photo Credits: Alexander Podshivalov/Dreamstime, cover; svetikd/iStock, 1; Gagandeep Ghuman/iStock, 3; Anna Kucherova/Shutterstock, 4, 5 (background); Cineberg/iStock, 5 (foreground); Kamran Jebreili/AP Images, 6-7; cherezoff/Shutterstock, 8 (background); Mega Pixel/Shutterstock, 8 (foreground); Dragon Images/Shutterstock, 9; KathyDewar/iStock, 10-11 (foreground); Radoslaw Lecyk/Shutterstock, 10-11 (background); C.C. Lockwood/Age Fotostock, 12-13; shigemi okano/Shutterstock, 14-15; RaksyBH/Shutterstock, 16-17; Cineberg/Shutterstock, 18 (left); Unkas Photo/Shutterstock, 18 (right); RosaIreneBetancourt 6/Alamy, 19; TTstudio/Shutterstock, 20-21; Haveseen/Dreamstime, 23.

Printed in the United States of America at Corporate Graphics in North Mankato, Minnesota.

TABLE OF CONTENTS

CHAPTER 1
ENGINEERED FOR SAFETY

This is the tallest **skyscraper** in the world. It is the Burj Khalifa in Dubai! It is 2,717 feet (828 meters) tall! **Engineers** designed it.

Burj Khalifa

They made this building safe from wind. Wind pushes tall buildings. They move slightly from side to side. This is called sway. **Earthquakes** can cause sway, too.

How do they build for sway? Sometimes, they design buildings with special shapes. The Burj Khalifa has a Y-shaped base. It is very **stable**. It can stand up to strong winds.

Special building materials help, too. The core is made of strong concrete. Concrete and steel are commonly used to build skyscrapers. Why? They can support a lot of weight.

base

CHAPTER 2

WEATHER AND DISASTERS

Engineers plan ahead. They plan for **natural disasters**, dangerous weather, and accidents. There is a lot to think about! They must follow **building codes**, too.

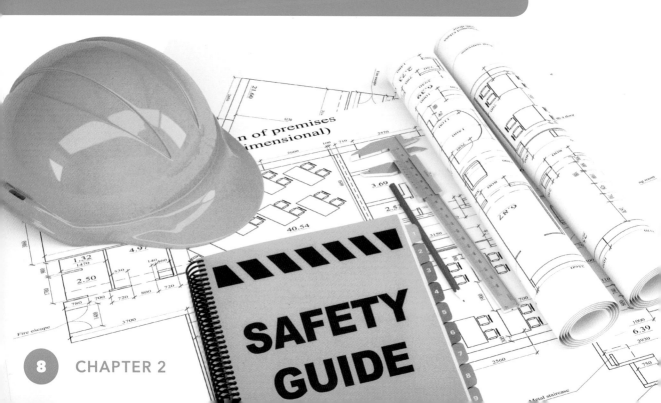

hazard map ····▶

Engineers look at hazard maps.
Why? They see where buildings
are most at risk for disaster.
Then they choose building materials.
They might make special designs.

Wildfires can burn down homes. Engineers help. How? They design with non-flammable materials. These include stucco, brick, and steel. Double-paned windows help keep flames out.

stucco

dome

Hurricanes bring strong winds and rain. **Tornadoes** do, too. **Reinforced** roofs help. They connect to the walls of a home. This helps keep the roof from blowing off. Windows can be made with stronger glass, too.

This home has a dome-shaped roof. Wind flows over it. It can't lift the roof off.

DID YOU KNOW?

Tornadoes bring strong winds! They can blow up to 300 miles (483 kilometers) per hour. That is twice as fast as hurricane winds!

shock absorber

Some areas have many earthquakes. Buildings must withstand shaking. **Shock absorbers** help. They are rubber. They absorb the movement. This keeps the building steady. Some are in the frame. Some are deep in the building's **foundation**.

TAKE A LOOK!

How do tall buildings withstand earthquakes? Take a look!

WEIGHTS
reduce movement

STEEL FRAME
strong and **flexible**

FOUNDATION

SHOCK ABSORBERS

BEDROCK

stilt ·····▶

Storms can cause flooding. Stilts help buildings stay dry. These raise the building above the ground. Openings on lower floors are sealed. This stops water from getting in.

CHAPTER 3

STAYING SAFE

Building inspectors visit homes and buildings. Why? They make sure buildings follow codes.

Some buildings are not built for bad weather. People make changes before big storms. Like what? They board up windows. They bolt doors shut.

New York City

We keep building taller buildings. In 1910, the tallest building was 700 feet (213 m) high. Now it is just one of many tall buildings in New York City!

Builders want to make a building taller than the Burj Khalifa. How do you think they will do it safely?

DID YOU KNOW?

Zap! Lightning rods keep tall buildings safe during storms. How? The rods collect the lightning's **energy**. This stops fires from starting.

ACTIVITIES & TOOLS

TEST YOUR OWN BUILDING

Engineers test out building designs with models. This helps them plan for natural disasters. You can make your own model. See if it can stand up to an earthquake!

What You Need:
- toothpicks
- miniature marshmallows
- small pieces of cardboard
- clear tape
- aluminum baking pan
- 1 box of instant gelatin

❶ Using the toothpicks, marshmallows, and cardboard, make a model building. Will you build a tall skyscraper or a short, sturdy building?

❷ Make the gelatin in a flat pan. Allow it to set.

❸ When the gelatin is ready, place your model on top. Gently move the pan back and forth. Does your building hold up? Does it fall?

❹ Go back to the drawing board to design and test new models until you create a structure that stays intact!

GLOSSARY

building codes: Rules and regulations engineers and builders have to follow to make and keep structures safe.

building inspectors: Professionals who examine buildings to see if they meet building code requirements.

earthquakes: Sudden shakings of the ground, often due to a release of energy deep within Earth.

energy: The ability of something to do work.

engineers: People who design systems, structures, products, or machines.

flexible: Able to bend.

foundation: The underground structure that supports a building.

hurricanes: Violent tropical storms with heavy rain and high winds.

natural disasters: Sudden events in nature that cause serious damage or loss of life.

reinforced: Strengthened or supported, usually with material.

shock absorbers: Devices that absorb the energy of shocks or vibrations in structures.

skyscraper: A very tall building with many stories.

stable: Created in a way that resists forces of change or motion.

tornadoes: Violent wind storms that appear as dark, funnel-shaped clouds.

wildfires: Large and very destructive fires, usually in rural or wilderness areas.

TO LEARN MORE

Finding more information is as easy as 1, 2, 3.

❶ Go to www.factsurfer.com

❷ Enter "safebuildings" into the search box.

❸ Choose your cover to see a list of websites.

FACT SURFER